The LOGIC *of* ENGLISH

The Phonogram and Spelling Game Book

by DENISE EIDE

PEDIALEARNING
INCORPORATED

Table of Contents

Introduction

Phonograms are the foundation of reading, and reading is the foundation of all academics. It is important that students learn the phonograms to mastery. The only way to accomplish this is through repetition over time.

The Phonogram and Spelling Game Book provides a variety of active and fun ways to drill phonograms and practice spelling. Too often teachers do not provide students with adequate practice to achieve mastery because it is assumed that drill is boring. In addition, teachers struggle to retain their students' attention. The activities in this book are meant to break that myth and demonstrate that it is possible to drill while respecting students' needs for variety.

The activities also are designed to engage all the learning styles. Teachers and parents of kinesthetic students will find many of the activities beneficial to engaging their active students.

Most of the materials needed are included with *The Phonogram and Spelling Game Book*. Teachers are allowed to make copies of the masters included in the Appendix for use by their direct students.

Other suggested materials include: three sets of *Logic of English Game Cards* and one set of Phonogram Flash Cards. These cards are available for purchase at www.LogicOfEnglish.com.

Chapter 1

Phonogram Card Games

These games require 1-3 sets of The Logic of English Game Cards.
Cards are available in blue bookface type, red manuscript, and green cursive.
To purchase, visit us at www.LogicOfEnglish.com.

Phonogram Memory

Players: 2-6

Supplies Needed: 2 decks of phonogram game cards. Choose matching pairs of 10-15 phonograms.

Directions:

»   Mix the phonogram cards. Lay all the cards face down in rows in the middle of the table.

»   The first player chooses a card and flips it upright so everyone may see. He then reads the sounds.

»   The player then chooses a second card, flips it upright, and reads the sounds.

»   If the phonograms match, he keeps the pair and goes again.

»   If the phonograms do not match, he flips them back to face down and play passes to the next player.

»   Play ends when all the pieces are matched. The player with the most sets wins.

Variation 1:   Work as a team against the clock to find the matches.

Variation 2:   Use lowercase and uppercase sandpaper letters. When a student flips a card, he must read the sound(s) and write them with his index finger.

Phonogram Snatch

Players: 1-2 players, 1 dealer/caller.

Supplies Needed: 1 deck of phonogram game cards, including the phonograms desired for review.

Directions:

»   Direct students to sit in a line, with the dealer/caller in the middle.

»   The dealer lays out 4-8 phonogram cards face up in a grid on the table.

»   The dealer then reads 1 of the phonogram sound(s), including spelling aid. Players race to snatch the card.

»   The first person to snatch it keeps it.

»   The dealer then replaces the card and calls out a new sound(s).

» Play continues until all the phonograms have been snatched.

» The winner is the player with the most cards.

Variation 1:   Use sandpaper letters instead of phonogram cards. When the student snatches the phonogram, he must write the letter with his finger and repeat the sounds.

Variation 2:   Say only one sound. Students are to snatch all the phonograms which share that sound.

Go Fish!

Players: 2-6

Supplies Needed: 2 decks of phonogram game cards. Choose 20-40 matching phonogram pairs, depending upon ages of students and size of group.

Directions:

» Deal 4-7 cards per player.

» Place the remaining cards in the middle of the table face down and spread them out into a "fishing pond."

» The first player chooses another player to ask, "Do you have a ___?" Students should ask for the phonograms by sound(s) and spelling aid.

» If the answer is "yes," he gives it to the asking player who then lays it down as a match. The asking player then repeats his turn.

» If the answer is "no," he should tell the asking player, "Go fish." The asking player then draws a card from the pond. If a match is found, it is laid down and the asking player repeats his turn.

» If no match is found, play moves to the next player on the left.

» Continue to play until all the cards have been matched.

» The player with the most matches wins.

Variation: Include 3 or 4 matches of each phonogram card in the pile. Students must then find sets of 3 or 4 in order to lay them down.

Dragon

Players: 2-6

Supplies Needed: 2 decks of phonogram game cards and 1 *Dragon* card. Choose a set of 20-40 matching phonogram pairs, depending upon the ages of students and size of group.

Directions:

» Deal out all the cards to the players. Some players may have 1 more or 1 less card than others.

» Players look through their hand and lay down any matches. As they lay down a match, they must read the sounds.

» Players should hold their cards in a fan in their hand.

» To begin play, the first player chooses another player from whom to draw a card. If a match is found, the sound(s) are read, the match is laid down, and the player takes another turn.

» If a match is not found, play moves to the next player on the left.

» Play ends when someone lays down all his cards.

» The player left holding the *Dragon* card loses.

Phonogram Slap

Players: 2-8

Supplies Needed: 3 decks of phonogram game cards. Choose 13-15 phonograms to practice for every 4 players. Use 3 of each phonogram. 3 *Slap* cards.

Directions:

Deal out all the cards to the players. Some players may have 1 more or 1 less card than others.

» Players should place their cards in a stack upside down in front of them.

» The first player flips the top card in his stack into the middle so that all players may see it and reads the sound(s).

» The second player flips his first card and places it on top of the stack, reads the sound(s), and so forth.

» If the *Slap* card is flipped, players race to slap it. Whoever slaps the *Slap* card first wins the entire stack of cards. He then places the cards under his stack and begins the play again.

» If 2 matching cards are laid down on top of each other or separated by only 1 card, players race to slap the deck. The player must then read the phonogram sound(s). If the player does not know the sounds, the other players have another opportunity to slap the pile and try again. The first player to slap the pile and read the sound(s) correctly takes the cards.

» The game is won when 1 player has possession of all the cards.

Variation 1:   Students may slap any pair of phonograms which have 1 or more sounds in common. Students must state which sound is shared in order to take the stack.

Speed

Players: 2-4, 1 Reader

Supplies Needed: 2-3 decks of phonogram game cards, and 1 set of phonogram flash cards. Choose 10-30 phonograms to practice.

Directions:

» Choose a reader.

» Mix the set of phonogram flash cards. Place the cards face down in front of the reader.

» Mix 2-3 decks of phonogram game cards together.

» Deal all the cards evenly to each player. Extra cards begin the discard pile. (Do not deal any to the reader.)

» Players hold their cards in their hand so that they may see them.

» The reader selects the top card from the stack in front of him and reads the sound(s) and spelling aid aloud.

» Players look at their cards. Those with a match race to lay it on top of the discard pile in the center. The first person to get the card to the center is allowed to discard. Others must put the card back into their hands.

» The reader may then replace the card anywhere in his reading stack and reads the next phonogram.

» The first person to discard all his cards wins.

Variation: When the reader calls a sound, everyone discards the card. The reader then places the used cards aside.

Last One!

Players: 2-6

Supplies Needed: 2-3 decks of phonogram game cards each in a different color, 2 *Wild* cards, 2 *Draw Two* cards, 2 *Reverse* cards. Choose matching sets of 10-15 phonograms to practice.

Directions:

»   Shuffle the cards chosen from the 2-3 decks of phonogram game cards together.

»   Deal 7 cards to each player.

»   Place the remaining cards face down in the middle of the table as the draw pile.

»   Turn 1 card face up to form the discard pile.

»   Play begins by a player discarding a card that matches the card on the discard pile either in color or in phonogram. The student must read the phonogram sound(s) as he discards.

»   If the player misreads the sound(s), he forfeits his turn and play moves to the next player.

»   If a player does not have a matching card, he must draw 1 card from the draw pile. Play then continues with the next player.

»   Players may play a *Draw Two* or *Reverse* card only if it matches in color.

»   If a *Draw Two* is played, the next person must draw 2 cards from the draw pile. He may not lay down a card.

»   If a *Reverse* card is played, the play switches directions.

»   If a *Wild* card is played, the player may select a new color.

»   A player wins when he has discarded all his cards.

Variation 1:   For simpler play, remove the *Reverse* and/or *Draw Two* cards.

Variation 2:   To increase the challenge, add the *Stack* card to the deck. When a *Stack* card is played, the player may play all the phonograms in his hand which share one or more sound(s) with the phonogram on the discard pile.

Rotten Egg

Players: 2-12

Supplies Needed: 1 deck of phonogram game cards, a cloth bag to hold them, 1-3 *Rotten Egg* cards, depending upon the difficulty.

Directions:

» Place all the phonogram cards in the bag with the 1-3 *Rotten Egg* cards.

» Set the timer for an undisclosed time of 2-3 minutes.

» Students take turns drawing a card and reading the phonogram aloud.

» If they get it right, they keep the card and pass the bag.

» If they do not read the phonogram correctly, they must put it back in the bag and pass the bag to the next person.

» If a student draws the *Rotten Egg*, he must put all his cards back into the bag and pass it to the next player.

» Play ends when the timer beeps. The student holding the most cards wins.

Variation 1:   Add a *Snatch It* card to the bag. If a student draws the *Snatch It* card, he may take the cards of any other player.

Variation 2:   Add a *Lose It* card to the bag. If a student draws the *Lose It* card, he must give his cards to the player on his left.

Team Up

Players: 2-3 teams of students. Two students per team.

Supplies Needed: 1 deck of phonogram game cards, 2 *Wild* cards, 2 *Go Back 1 Space* cards, 2 *Go Back 2 Spaces* cards, 1 *Return to Go* card, and 1 game board (page 63 or 64). Each team will also need: 1 small whiteboard, 1 dry erase marker, 1 eraser, and a game board piece to mark progress along the board.

Directions:

» To set up the game:
  - Mix the phonogram game cards with the additional game cards. Place them face side down in a draw pile alongside the edge of the board.
  - Provide each team with a whiteboard, dry erase marker, and eraser.
  - Place the game pieces on Start.

» Play will alternate between teams.
  - To begin, Player A on Team 1 draws a card without showing his teammate. He then reads the phonogram sound(s) and spelling aids from memory. Player B must write the phonogram correctly.
  - Team 2 checks that the phonogram was read and spelled correctly and awards 1 point to Team 1 for correct reading and 1 point to Team 1 for correct spelling. The team advances their piece accordingly.
  - If the phonogram was read incorrectly, no points are awarded.

» Play then moves to Team 2.

» If a *Wild* card is drawn, the team advances 1 space and the turn is passed to the next team.

» If a *Go Back 1 Space* or *Go Back 2 Spaces* card is drawn, the team must follow the directions and play passes to the next team.

» If a *Return to Go* card is drawn, the team must move their game piece back to the beginning.

» The team to reach End first wins.

Variation 1:   Eliminate the *Return to Go* card.

Variation 2:   Write spelling words on index cards and use these instead of phonogram game cards. Students must then read and spell the words.

Chapter 2

Active Phonogram Games

These games involve large motor skill movement.
They provide a fun and engaging way to practice for active learners.

Phonogram Baseball

Players: 1+

Supplies Needed: Phonogram game cards or flash cards, whiteboard, marker, 3 bases, and a home plate.

Directions:

- » Choose the location for home plate and 3 bases.

- » The student "up to bat" stands on home plate with a whiteboard and marker.

- » The teacher chooses a phonogram card and reads it to the batter.

- » The batter writes the phonogram on his whiteboard.
  - · If it is spelled correctly, he advances to the next base.
  - · If it is not spelled correctly, he is "out."

- » At each base, he is given another phonogram to spell.

- » 3 outs and the game is over.

- » Each time he crosses home plate, he is awarded 1 point.

Variation 1:

- » With more than 1 player, there can be multiple batters. All the batters begin at the same time on home. All of the players need a whiteboard and marker.

- » When the teacher reads the phonogram, the batters writes it.

- » If the player spells it correctly, he advances to the next base.

- » If he does not spell it correctly, he receives his first "out" and returns to home.

- » 3 outs and the player is out of the game. The winner is the last player remaining.

Variation 2:

- » Divide players into teams. 1 team will need be up to bat; the other team will be the pitcher.

- » The student "up to bat" stands on home plate with a whiteboard and marker.

- » The pitcher chooses a phonogram card and reads it to the batter and any runners on base.

- » The batter and runners write the phonogram on their whiteboards.
  - · Whoever spells it correctly advances to the next base.
  - · If it is not spelled correctly, that player is out.

- » Each time a player crosses home plate, his team is awarded 1 point.

- » 3 outs and the teams switch roles.

- » Play an agreed upon number of innings.

The Phonogram Circuit

Players: 1-4

Supplies Needed: 1 set of phonogram game cards or flash cards. Whiteboards or paper at 4 stations around the room, whiteboard marker or pencil.

Directions:

» At a designated starting place, show the student a phonogram. The student reads the phonogram sound(s), then runs to station 1 to write it and shout the sounds, then to station 2 to write it and shout the sounds, then to station 3, etc.

» When he returns to the starting point, he is given a new phonogram.

Variation 1: Set a timer. See how many phonograms he can write correctly in 3 minutes.

Variation 2: Set the students up in relay teams. When the player returns to start, the next player on the team goes.

Last One Standing

Players: 2+

Supplies Needed: Whiteboard and whiteboard marker for each student.

Directions:

» Direct all the students to stand up.

» Read a phonogram sound(s) and spelling aid.

» Students write it on their whiteboard.

  • If the students write it correctly, they remain standing.
  • If the students write it incorrectly, they sit down.

» The last student standing wins.

Phonogram Hop

Players: 1-4

Supplies Needed: 1 set of phonogram game cards or flash cards, and a bean bag.

Directions:

- » Lay the phonogram cards out in a hopscotch shape on the floor.

- » Direct students to stand at the beginning.

- » The first student tosses the bean bag to a phonogram. She then hops to the phonogram card, reads the sounds, picks it up and hops back.

- » If the incorrect sounds are read she may not pick up the phonogram card and play passes to the next player.

- » The student with the most phonogram cards at the end wins.

Variation 1:   Eliminate the bean bag. The teacher reads a phonogram sound(s) and spelling aid. Students must jump to the correct phonogram, repeat the sounds, pick it up, and hop back.

Phonogram Treasure Hunt

Players: 1+

Supplies Needed: 1 set of phonogram game cards or flash cards.

Directions:

- » When the students are not looking, hide the phonogram cards around the room.

- » Direct students to find the hidden phonogram cards.

- » When each card is found, he must bring it to the teacher and read the sound(s).

Phonogram Mountain

Players: 1-2

Supplies Needed: 1 set of phonogram game cards or flash cards and a stairway.

Directions:

- » Direct students to stand at the bottom of the mountain (stairs).

- » The teacher then stands at the top. She shows a student a phonogram.
  - If the student reads it correctly, he advances 1 step.
  - If the student reads it incorrectly, he goes down 1 step.
- » The game is finished when the student reaches the top step.

Variation 1:   Students advance up the number of steps based upon the number of sounds read correctly. For example "a" has three sounds.

Phonogram Tag

Players: 1

Supplies Needed: 1 set of phonogram game cards or flash cards.

Directions:

- » Direct the student to stand at a designated starting place in the room.

- » The teacher stands an agreed upon distance away.

- » The teacher shows a phonogram to the student.
  - If the student reads it correctly, he advances 1 step toward the teacher.
  - If the student reads it incorrectly, the teacher retreats 1 step backward.
- » The game is finished when the student tags the teacher.

Variation 1:   This game may be played with 2 students.

Phonogram Kangaroo

Players: 1-4

Supplies Needed: 1 deck of phonogram game cards per student. Select the cards the students are working on at this time. Optional: a tail to tie to each student to transform him into a kangaroo.

Directions:

» Lay the phonograms on the floor in a random pattern.

» Call out a phonogram sound. Students are to jump to the phonogram in one giant leap.

The Phonogram Tightrope

Players: 1+

Supplies Needed: 1 set of phonogram game cards or flash cards. A string laid along the floor, or line taped on the carpet for each student.

Directions:

» Direct students to stand at the beginning of the string/tape.

» Show the students the phonogram card.

» To advance 1 heel to toe step, he must read the sound(s) correctly.

  · If the phonogram makes more than 1 sound, he may take a step for each sound.
  · If he falls off the tightrope, he must go back to the beginning.

» When students are waiting for each other, they must stand still on their "tightropes."

Phonogram Maze

Players: 1

Supplies Needed: 1 set of phonogram game cards or flash cards.

Directions:

» Lay the phonogram cards on the floor in a maze snaking throughout the room.

» Show the student which end is the start and which end is the finish.

» Call out a phonogram sound(s) and spelling aid that is within reach of the student. It may be a small or large step. The student is to step to that phonogram without touching any of the others. When he arrives, he must repeat the sound(s).

» The student follows the phonogram maze until he reaches the end.

Variation 1:   The student stands at the beginning of the maze and he calls out the sound(s) of the phonogram he will advance to, then steps to the phonogram and continues.

Move It!

Players: 1+

Supplies Needed: 1 set of phonogram game cards or flash cards.

Directions:

» Show students a phonogram card. For each sound read correctly, he may jump, do a jumping jack, a somersault on the floor, or other agreed upon action.

Phonogram Basketball

Players: 1-4 or relay teams

Supplies Needed: Slips of paper for writing phonograms, 1 pencil per student, 1 basket per student or per team, and phonogram cards (or list) for teacher to read.

Directions:

> » Read a phonogram sound(s).

> » Students write the phonogram on a slip of paper.

> » If the phonogram was written correctly, he may crumple it up and try to make a basket.

> » Award one point for writing the phonogram correctly, and one point per basket.

> » The student with the most points wins.

Variation 1:

> » Select 15-20 phonograms to practice.

> » Read all the phonograms while students write them on slips of paper.

> » When all the sounds are written, set students up with a basket.

> » Call out a phonogram sound. Students must shuffle through their slips until they find the correct one.

> » They must then crumple it up and toss it into the basket.

> » The student that makes the most baskets wins.

Variation 2:   Say a word, ask the student to find the phonogram that represents the spelling of the first sound. Continue as directed above.

Variation 3:   Set up a 1–point line, 2–point line, and 3–point line from which to try to make a basket.

Phonogram Sky Writing

Players: 1+

Supplies Needed: 1 set of phonogram game cards or flash cards.

Directions:

» Direct students to stand.

» Choose a phonogram card. Read the phonogram sound(s) and spelling aid.

» Direct students to write the phonogram in large motions in the air.

Blind Writing

Players: 1+

Supplies Needed: 1 set of phonogram game cards or flash cards, whiteboard, markers, and eraser.

Directions:

» Provide students with a whiteboard, marker, and eraser.

» Read a phonogram sound(s) and spelling aid.

» Direct students to write the phonogram on the whiteboard with their eyes closed.

Back Writing

Players: 2

Supplies Needed: 1 set of phonogram game cards or flash cards.

Directions:

» A student chooses a phonogram card.

» He then writes the phonogram on the back of the other person. The other person then tries to guess which phonogram is being written.

Snatch the Match!

Players: 1+

Supplies Needed: 2 decks of phonogram game cards, obstacles.

Directions:

» Place 1 deck of phonogram cards on 1 side of the room. Place the second deck of phonogram cards on the other side of the room.

» If desired, set up an obstacle course between the 2 sets.

» The student must go to the first deck of phonogram game cards, pick 1, read it aloud, then race around the obstacles to the second set of cards, find the matching phonogram, run to the teacher, say the sound(s) and begin again.

» Play stops when all phonograms have been matched.

Variation 1:   Set a timer. Challenge students to see how many sets they can make in 2 minutes, 3 minutes, etc.

Variation 2:   Time how long it takes to match all the sets.

Variation 3:   Set up 2 courses. Direct students to race each other.

Variation 4:   Play the game as a relay. Divide students into teams. 1 student goes at a time. After reading the phonogram to the teacher, they must tag the next student in line. Teams may race for 2 minutes to see who can get the most phonograms, or they may race on 2 separate courses.

Variation 5:   Use the lowercase and uppercase sandpaper letters. Students must read and "write" the phonogram before continuing.

Chapter 3

Other Phonogram Games

*Many of these games use the masters available in Appendix One.
Phonogram Bingo and Tic-Tac-Toe game masters
are available to print, starting on page 69.*

Phonogram Bingo

Players: 1+

Supplies Needed: 1 set of Bingo cards from pages 70-87 or use the blank master on page 58 to create your own. 1 set of phonogram game cards or flash cards. (Choose either A-Z or the multi-letter phonograms.) Pennies or other small objects to cover the phonograms.

Directions:

» Decide if students must have 5 in a row or cover the whole board.

» Provide students with a Bingo chart.

» The caller chooses a phonogram card and calls out the sound(s) and spelling aid.

» Students cover the phonogram on their Bingo chart as the sound(s) are called.

» When a student has 5 in a row (or the whole board) covered, he should call out, "Bingo!"

» The student must then read the phonogram sounds back to check them.

Variation 1:   Provide students with a blank Bingo card (page 58). Dictate the phonograms while students write them in any order on the card. Then play Bingo as directed above.

Variation 2:   Play Speed Bingo. The caller reads the phonograms quickly while the players try to cover the spaces on their cards.

Phonogram Tic-Tac-Toe

Players: 2

Supplies Needed: Phonogram Tic-Tac-Toe cards (Tic-Tac-Toe masters are available on pages 88-96).

Directions:

» Pairs of students play Tic-Tac-Toe. In order to cross out the square, they must read the sound(s) correctly.

Variation 1:   Provide students with a blank Tic-Tac-Toe card (page 60). Dictate the phonograms for the students to write on the board. Play Tic-Tac-Toe as directed above.

Phonogram Flip

Players: 1

Supplies Needed: 1 Phonogram Flip game card per student (page 61), cut on the dotted lines. 2 dice per student.

Directions:

» Dictate 12 phonograms for the student to write in any order on the Phonogram Flip game card.

» The student rolls the dice. He then reads the phonogram written by the number shown on the dice.

- If he reads it correctly, he flips the flap closed and rolls again.
- If he reads it incorrectly, he may not close the flap and rolls again.

» The game is over when all the flaps are closed.

Beat the Clock

Players: 1+

Supplies Needed: 1 set of 74 phonogram cards and a stop watch.

Directions:

» Direct students to read the phonograms as quickly as possible. Read the sounds only without the spelling aids.

» Keep a record of the fastest time.

Eraser Race

Players: 1+

Supplies Needed: Large whiteboard, marker, and eraser.

Directions:

> » The teacher begins to write phonograms on the whiteboard as quickly as possible.

> » When a student reads 1 correctly, the teacher must erase it, while continuing to try to write faster than the students are reading.

> » When the students catch the teacher, the game is over.

Variation 1:   The class decides upon a handicap for the teacher and allows the teacher to write an agreed upon number of phonograms before they begin to read.

Phonogram Telephone

Players: 2+

Supplies Needed: 1 set of phonogram game cards or flash cards, 1 whiteboard, marker, and eraser.

Directions:

> » Students sit in a line.

> » The first student in line draws a phonogram card and without showing it to anyone, whispers the sound(s) and spelling aid to the next person in line.

> » The next person whispers it to the next. . . .

> » The final person in line writes the phonogram on the whiteboard.

Phonogram Blitz

Players: 1+

Supplies Needed: 1 blank Blitz card per player (page 59). 1 set of 25 phonogram cards. Small objects to cover the Blitz squares.

Directions:

» Students may select any 1 spot on the Blitz card as a free spot.

» The teacher reads the phonogram sound(s) and spelling aids in random order.

» As the teacher calls out a sound, students choose a square on the Blitz card to write the phonogram.

» Once all the squares are filled, the teacher mixes the phonogram cards in random order.

» The teacher then begins to call out the phonogram sound(s) and spelling aids as quickly as possible while the students search their boards and cover the phonograms that have been called.

» Students are to call "Blitz" when they have covered 5 in a row.

» When students call "Blitz," they must read the phonogram sounds back to check them.

Variation 1:   Have a student play the role of the teacher.

Teacher Trouble

Players: 1+

Supplies Needed: Phonogram game cards or flash cards, bell or buzzer for the student to ring when the teacher is in error.

Directions:

» The teacher explains that today she has forgotten her phonograms and she needs the students to drill her.

» Students show her the phonogram cards and the teacher reads the sound(s) and says the spelling aid.

» When she gets one incorrect, the students ring the bell or buzzer.

Alphabetical Order Race

Players: 2+, or divide into teams

Supplies Needed: 1 set of phonogram game cards or flash cards per student or team.

Directions:

» Provide each student or team with a set of phonogram cards in random order. When the teacher says "Go," each team attempts to arrange the cards in ABC order as fast as possible.

Variation 1: Use the sandpaper letters, either lowercase or uppercase.

Phonogram Board Game

Players: 1+

Supplies Needed: Blank phonogram game board (page 63 or 64), 1 game piece per student to advance along the board, and 1 die per student.

Directions:

» Dictate 34 phonograms while the students write them in the spaces on the game board. They may write them in any order.

» When the board is filled, the student rolls the die and advances the correct number of spaces. The student must read each of the phonograms he passes.
  - If the phonograms are read correctly, the student may stay at that spot.
  - If a phonogram is not read correctly, the student rolls the die again and goes backwards the number of spaces shown.

Variation 1: If a student rolls a 3, he must go back 3 spaces.

Chapter 4

Phonogram Drills

In addition to games, phonograms may be drilled in a variety of ways. Many of these drills are much faster than playing a game and are therefore good for days when time is limited.

Reading Drill

Supplies Needed: 1 set of phonogram game cards or flash cards.

Directions:

» Students read the phonograms with or without spelling aids.

Variation 1:   Read them in a silly voice, whisper, shout, etc.

Variation 2:   Practice reading and writing using the sandpaper letters.

See it, Say it, Write it

Supplies Needed: 1 set of phonogram game cards or flash cards, whiteboard, marker, and eraser.

Directions:

» Place a stack of phonogram cards in front of the student.

» Direct students to draw a phonogram from the pile.

» He is then to read the phonogram and write it on the whiteboard.

Hear it, Write it

Supplies Needed: 1 set of phonogram game cards or flash cards, something for the student(s) to write on.

Directions:

» The teacher draws a phonogram card and reads the sound(s) and spelling aids.

» Students write the phonogram on a whiteboard, chalkboard, paper, etc.

Chapter 5

Sensory Practice

*Many students benefit from writing practice
that includes a sensory experience of the letters.*

Tactile Letters

These are an inexpensive alternative to purchased sandpaper letters.

Supplies Needed: Tactile letter templates (page 62), glitter glue.

Directions:

- »   Print the templates onto card stock.

- »   To make a set of tactile phonograms, write each letter with glitter glue onto the template. Allow to dry.

- »   When dry, allow students to feel the shape of each letter and practice the motions for letter formation.

Variation 1:   Rather than using glitter glue, draw the letters with school glue, then cover with sand.

Salt Box

Supplies Needed: Tray or shallow box. Salt to cover the bottom.

Directions:

- »   Call out a phonogram sound. Students write it in the salt.

Variation 1:   The salt may be replaced with flour, corn meal, whipped cream, pudding, or shaving cream.

Variation 2:   Put tempera paint in a ziplock bag. Close the bag tightly. Dictate phonograms as students write them with their index finger on the bag.

Chapter 6

Spelling Word Card Games

These games use spelling word cards. Before playing these games, direct students to write the target spelling words on index cards and use these cards to play the games as directed in the chapter.

Timed Reading Drill

Players: 1+

Supplies Needed: 1 set of spelling word cards per student, timer.

Directions:

- » Set the timer.

- » Direct students to read each card as quickly as possible.

- » When students have finished the stack, challenge them to read the cards a second time and see if they can beat their time.

Spelling Snap

Players: 1+

Supplies Needed: Each student will need 1 set of spelling word cards, 1-3 cards with *Snap* written on it, pencil, and paper. The teacher will need a timer.

Directions:

- » Place the spelling word cards in a pile face down in front of each student.

- » Provide each student with a piece of paper and pencil.

- » Mix 1-3 *Snap* cards into the stack.

- » Set a timer for an agreed amount of time from 1-3 minutes.

- » When the teacher says "go," the students flip a card, read it, write it, and flip another, until the timer runs out. If a *Snap* card is drawn, all the spelling cards go back into the pile and the student begins again. The *Snap* card is returned to the bottom of the pile.

- » Stop when the timer rings.

- » Students receive 2 points for each word spelled correctly and 1 point for each card face up.

- » The student with the most points wins.

Guess My Word

Players: 2+

Supplies Needed: 1 set of spelling word cards per class. Each student will need a small whiteboard, marker, and eraser.

Directions:

> » Choose 1 student to go to the front of the class.

> » The student in front chooses a spelling word card and describes the word aloud without saying the actual word.

> » Students must write their guesses on a whiteboard and display it to the student in front.

> » When a student guesses the word and spells it correctly, it is his turn to describe a new word.

Variation 1:   This game may be played like 20 questions. The guessing students ask yes/no questions to try to determine the word. To make an official guess, they must write it on a whiteboard and spell it correctly.

Speed Writing

Players: 1+

Supplies Needed: Each student will need 1 set of spelling word cards, paper, and a pencil. The teacher will need a timer.

Directions:

> » Place the spelling word cards in a pile in front of each student.

> » Provide each student with paper and pencil.

> » When the teacher says, "go," students flip the first card and begin to write the word as many times as possible.

> » Every 10-20 seconds, the teacher calls out, "flip."

> » Students flip a new card and write the the new word as many times as possible.

Variation 1:   When all the words have been written, guide students in evaluating the handwriting and choosing the best sample of each word. Evaluate words based upon size, balance on the line, evenness, etc.

ABC Order

Players: 1+

Supplies Needed: Each student will need 1 set of spelling word cards.

Directions:

» Direct students to race to arrange the spelling words into ABC order as quickly as possible.

Variation 1:   Time the students.

Reading Go Fish

Players: 2-4

Supplies Needed: 2 matching sets of spelling word cards. Choose 10-20 spelling words, depending upon ages of students and size of group.

Directions:

» Deal 4-7 cards per player.

» Place the remaining cards in the middle of the table face down and spread them out into a "fishing pond."

» The first player chooses another player to ask, "Do you have a ___?"
  • If the answer is "yes," he gives it to the asking player who then lays it down as a match. The asking player then repeats his turn.
  • If the answer is "no," he should tell the asking player, "Go fish." The asking player then draws a card from the pond. If a match is found, it is laid down and the asking player repeats his turn.

» If no match is found, the player incorporates the cards into his hand and play moves to the next player on the left. Continue to play until all the cards have been matched.

» The player with the most matches wins.

Sort Those Words

Players: 1+

Supplies Needed: 1 set of spelling word cards per student.

Directions:

» Call out various ways for students to sort the words. For example: ABC order, words with silent final Es, words with long vowel sounds, words with the short vowel sound, nouns, verbs, etc.

Spelling Word Memory

Players: 2-6

Supplies Needed: 2 sets of spelling word cards.

Directions:

» Mix the spelling word cards. Lay all the cards face down in rows in the middle of the table.

» The first player chooses a card and flips it upright so everyone may see. He then reads the word.

» The player then chooses a second card, flips it upright, and reads the word.
  - If the words match, he keeps the pair and goes again.
  - If the words do not match, he flips them back to face down and play passes to the next player.

» Play ends when all the pieces are matched. The winner with the most sets wins.

Variation 1:   Work as a team against the clock to find the matches.

Compound Word Game

Players: 1+

Supplies Needed: 1 set of spelling word cards. Each card in the set should have a minimum of 1 other card in the set that together forms a compound word. Paper, pencil, and a timer.

Directions:

» Set the timer for 1-3 minutes.

» Students should match cards into compound words, writing down each word they find.

Variation 1:   For Group Play: distribute 2-3 cards to each student. They must walk around the room finding students with other words that form compound words. Each time a word is found, they must write it down. The student with the most compound words wins.

Chapter 7

Active Spelling Games

*The games in this chapter are a way to integrate
large motor skills with reading and spelling.*

Blind Spelling

Players: 2+

Supplies Needed: Each pair of students will need spelling word cards, whiteboard, marker, and eraser.

Directions:

> » Direct students to work in pairs at a whiteboard.

> » 1 student reads a practice word, the other writes it with his eyes closed.

Spelling Word Scavenger Hunt

Players: 2+

Supplies Needed: 1 set of spelling word cards. 1 whiteboard, marker, and eraser per pair of students.

Directions:

> » Distribute the spelling word cards around the room.

> » In pairs, students travel around the room finding the words. 1 student reads the word that is found. The other student writes it.
>   - If he spells it correctly without looking, the team receives 1 point.
>   - The players then switch roles and move on to find the next word.

> » The team with the most points wins.

Spelling Basketball

Players: 1+

Supplies Needed: Slips of paper for writing spelling words, 1 pencil per student, 1 basket per student or per team.

Directions:

» Read a spelling word aloud.

» Students write the word on a slip of paper.

» If the word is written correctly, he may crumple it up and try to make a basket.

» Award 1 point for writing the word correctly, and 1 point per basket.

» The student with the most points wins.

Variation 1:

» Select 15-20 words to practice.

» Read all the words while students write them on slips of paper.

» When all the words are written, set students up with a basket.

» Call out a word. Students must shuffle through their slips until they find the correct one.

» They must then crumple it up and toss it into the basket.

» The student that makes the most baskets wins.

Variation 2: Assign varying point values to the words based upon difficulty.

Spelling Baseball

Players: 1+

Supplies Needed: Spelling word cards, whiteboard, marker, 3 bases, and a home plate.

Directions:

» Choose the location for home plate and the 3 bases.

» The student "up to bat" stands on home plate with a whiteboard and marker.

» The teacher chooses a spelling word card and reads it to the batter.

» The batter writes the word on his whiteboard.
   - If it is spelled correctly, he advances to the next base.
   - If it is not spelled correctly, he is "out" and must return to home.

» At each base, he is given another word to spell.

» Each time he crosses home plate, he is awarded 1 point.

Variation 1:

» With more than 1 player, there can be multiple batters. All the batters begin at the same time on home. All of the players need a whiteboard and marker.

» When the teacher reads the word, the batters spell it.
   - If a player spells it correctly, he advances to the next base.
   - If he does not spell it correctly, he receives his first "out" and returns to home.

» 3 outs and the player is out of the game. The winner is the last player remaining.

Variation 2:

» Divide players into teams. 1 team will need be up to bat, the other team will be the pitcher.

» The student up to bat stands on home plate with a whiteboard and marker.

» The pitcher chooses a spelling word card and reads it to the batter and any runners on base.

» The batter and runners write the word on their whiteboards.
   - If a players spells the word correctly, he advances to the next base.
   - If it is not spelled correctly, he is out.

» Each time a team member crosses home plate, his team is awarded 1 point.

» 3 outs and the teams switch roles.

» Play an agreed upon number of innings.

The Spelling Circuit

Players: 1-4

Supplies Needed: 1 set of spelling word cards. Whiteboards or paper at 4 stations around the room.

Directions:

» At the designated starting place, show the student a word. The student reads the word, then runs to station 1 to write it and reads it aloud, then to station 2 to write it and reads it aloud, then to station 3, etc.

» When the student returns to the starting point, he is given a new word.

Variation 1:   Set a timer. See how many words he can write correctly in 3 minutes.

Variation 2:   Relay. Set the students up in teams. When the player returns to start, the next player on the team goes.

Sky Writing Words

Players: 1+

Supplies Needed: Spelling words.

Directions:

» Read a word.

» Students should write the word in large motions in the air while sounding it aloud.

Variation 1:   Students lie on their backs and write the words in the air using their feet.

Group Spelling

Players: 5+

Supplies Needed: Spelling words. 1 whiteboard, marker, and eraser per student.

Directions:

- » Students stand in a line or circle. Each student needs a whiteboard, marker, and eraser.
- » The teacher reads a word.
- » The first student in line writes the first phonogram in the word.
- » The second student in line writes the second phonogram, etc.

Variation 1:   If a student misspells a phonogram, he is out.

Variation 2:   Each student writes 1 letter on his whiteboard, rather than 1 phonogram.

Classroom Spelling

Players: 10+

Supplies Needed: 1 whiteboard, marker, and eraser per student.

Directions:

- » Dictate 1 phonogram per student. The student should write it on his whiteboard. (If students have a two-sided whiteboard, they may write a different phonogram on each side. Do not forget to give someone silent final E if it is needed.)
- » Call out a spelling word.
- » Students need to jump up and stand in line to collectively spell the word.

Chapter 8

Creative and Tactile Ideas for Spelling Practice

Rainbow Writing

Supplies Needed: Spelling words, blank paper, markers or colored pencils.

Directions:

» Read a word for students to practice spelling. Using different colors, the students then write the word on top of each word in 3 or more colors, creating a rainbow effect.

Texture Writing

Supplies Needed: Shaving cream, salt box, flour, pudding, whipped cream, play dough, etc.

Directions:

» Direct students to write their spelling words with their finger in shaving cream, a salt box, in flour, pudding, whipped cream, play dough, etc.

Variation 1:   Provide students with play dough and a pencil. Have them roll out the dough and carve the spelling words in the soft dough.

Variation 2:   Provide students with play dough. Have them roll the clay into strands and form the words with the clay.

Variation 3:   Provide students with play dough and alphabet cookie cutters. Direct them to write the spelling words with cut outs of each letter.

Picture Dictionary

Supplies Needed: Spelling words, paper, markers or colored pencils.

Directions:

» Direct students to write their spelling words on a page in alphabetical order and draw pictures to illustrate each word.

Variation 1:   Direct students to draw a scene which incorporates each spelling word in the picture. Students are then to label each spelling word within the picture.

Spelling Collage

Supplies Needed: List of spelling words, scissors, large piece of blank paper, glue, old magazines and newspapers with words and pictures that students may cut out.

Directions:

» Direct students to find the spelling words in print, or to cut out the letters and write the words using cut out letters. Paste the words onto blank paper.

» Students may add pictures that illustrate each spelling word.

Guess My Picture

Players: 2+

Supplies Needed: Spelling words, paper, markers, ruler.

Directions:

» Students draw 1 picture for each spelling word. Using a ruler, draw a line under the picture.

» Students then exchange pictures and write the spelling word that matches the drawing under each picture.

Word Picture

Supplies Needed: Spelling words, paper, markers.

Directions:

» Provide students with a line drawing. They write their spelling words following the outline of the picture.

Window Writing

Supplies Needed: Window paint, paint brush, window or mirror.

Directions:

» Direct students to practice writing their spelling words using window paint on a window or mirror.

Sentence Writing

Supplies Needed: Spelling words, paper, pencil.

Directions:

» Challenge students to write sentences incorporating as many of the spelling words as possible. The sentence must be a complete thought and make complete sense, though it may be silly.

Variation 1: Together with the students, assign a point value to each word in the spelling list. Words which are more difficult to use or spell are worth more points. Challenge students to write sentences that include the most points.

Story Writing

Supplies Needed: Spelling words, paper, pencil.

Directions:

» Challenge students to write a story incorporating all of the spelling words. Each sentence must be a complete thought and make complete sense.

Variation 1: Assign a theme to the story.

Variation 2: Have students use the spelling words to compose a poem or limerick.

Chapter 9

Spelling Games

*Many of the games in this chapter
use the blank line masters found in the Appendix.*

Word Search

Supplies Needed: 10-20 spelling words, 1 blank Word Search per student (page 65).

Directions:

- » Provide each student with a blank Word Search.
- » Direct students to write their spelling words on the lines below.
- » Then have them write their spelling words in the grid—1 letter per square..
- » Add random letters to fill in the grid.
- » Have students exchange word searches and find the words.

Sink & Spell

Players: 2

Supplies Needed: 5-10 spelling words, 2 Sink & Spell grids per student (page 66).

Directions:

- » 2 students should secretly write the spelling words on 1 of their own grids. The other grid is to be left blank.
- » Without showing the other student his grid, student A calls out a coordinate. For example: "3F."
- » Student B looks at his grid.
  - • If a letter is written in the coordinate, he tells student A the letter by name. Student A writes the letter on the blank grid.
  - • If no letter is written, he says, "miss." Student A crosses out the spot.
- » Play then passes to the next player.
- » When a student has found a word on the other player's board, he announces the word and the coordinates.
- » The first player to find and identify all the words on the other player's board wins.

Spelling Tic-Tac-Toe

Players: 2

Supplies Needed: Spelling words, 1 Tic-Tac-Toe grid (page 67) per pair of students, 1 whiteboard, marker, and eraser per student.

Directions:

» Students decide who will be X and who will be O.

» Each student picks a square. It can be the same square.

» The teacher reads 2 words, 1 for each student.

» The students write the word on their whiteboard.

- If they spell the word correctly, they mark their grid with an X or an O.
- If they misspell the word, they do not mark it.
- If they chose the same square and they both spell the word correctly, no one makes a mark.

» The first student with 3-in-a-row wins.

Create a Crossword Maze

Players: 1+

Supplies Needed: 10 spelling words, 1 piece of Spelling Crossword paper (page 68) per student.

Directions:

» Direct students to organize the spelling words on a page in crossword puzzle fashion.

Create a Crossword Puzzle

Players: 1+

Supplies Needed: 10 spelling words, 2 pieces of Spelling Crossword paper (page 68).

Directions:

» On the first sheet of Spelling Crossword paper, direct students to organize the spelling words on the page in crossword puzzle fashion. Number each word in the upper right hand corner of the first letter. This first sheet will be the answer key.

» On the second sheet of Spelling Crossword paper, students darken the lines around the spaces needed for the puzzle and number each word.

» On the lines provided below the puzzle, students then write a sentence for each spelling word, leaving a blank in the place of the word.

» Students should exchange the puzzle with another student. The answer key may be used to check the answers.

Spelling I-Spy

Players: 2+

Supplies Needed: Spelling list.

Directions:

» 1 student choses a spelling word. He provides a clue to which word he is thinking of by saying, "I spy a word that _____." For example: "I spy a word with two single-letter vowels." "I spy a word that has four consonants." "I spy a word that is the antonym for _____."

» Other students guess which word he spies.

Spelling Scramble

Players: 2+

Supplies Needed: 2 or more sets of phonogram game cards. (You may limit the cards to A-Z, or provide targeted phonograms.)

Directions:

- » Provide each team with 2 or more sets of cards.

- » Call out a spelling word. Students must locate the letters and arrange them correctly. The first team to spell it correctly wins 1 point.

Variation 1:   Use scrabble tiles or magnetic letters.

Spelling Detectives

Players: 5 +

Supplies Needed: Large whiteboard, 2-3 chairs, 2-3 small whiteboards, markers, and erasers.

Directions:

- » Pick 2-3 students to be spelling detectives. They are to sit in chairs with their backs to the large whiteboard and facing the rest of the class. Each student should have a small whiteboard and marker.

- » Write a spelling word on the large whiteboard behind them.

- » The students in the chairs take turns asking the class yes/no questions about the word.

- » When they have guessed the word, students are to write it on their small whiteboard and show the class.

- » If the word is correct (including spelling), the student chooses a new detective to take his place.

Type the Words

Supplies Needed: Spelling words, computer.

Directions:

» Students type their words.

Variation 1: Have students type the words from a recorded dictation.

Variation 2: Students create collages using the spelling words in a graphics program.

Record the Words

Supplies Needed: Spelling words, mp3 recorder.

Directions:

» Students record the spelling words which they are struggling with to create a personal spelling quiz.

» Students then listen to the recording and write each word.

You're My Editor

Supplies Needed: Large whiteboard.

Directions:

» Write the spelling words on the board.

» Ask students to close their eyes.

» Rewrite a few of the words with mistakes.

» Students need to look at the list and find the errors.

Variation 1: Write sentences on the board that include spelling, grammar, and punctuation errors. Challenge students to be your editor and find the mistakes.

Appendix A

Templates

Phonogram Bingo

Phonogram Blitz

Phonogram Tic-Tac-Toe

Phonogram Flip

1	
2	
3	
4	
5	
6	
7	
8	
9	
10	
11	
12	

Tactile Letter Templates

Game Board

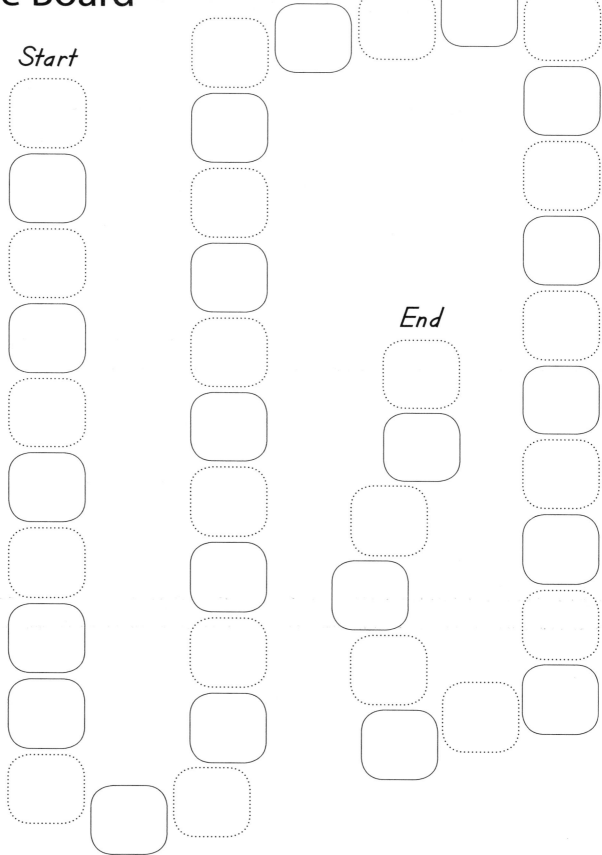

Start

End

Game Board

Start

End

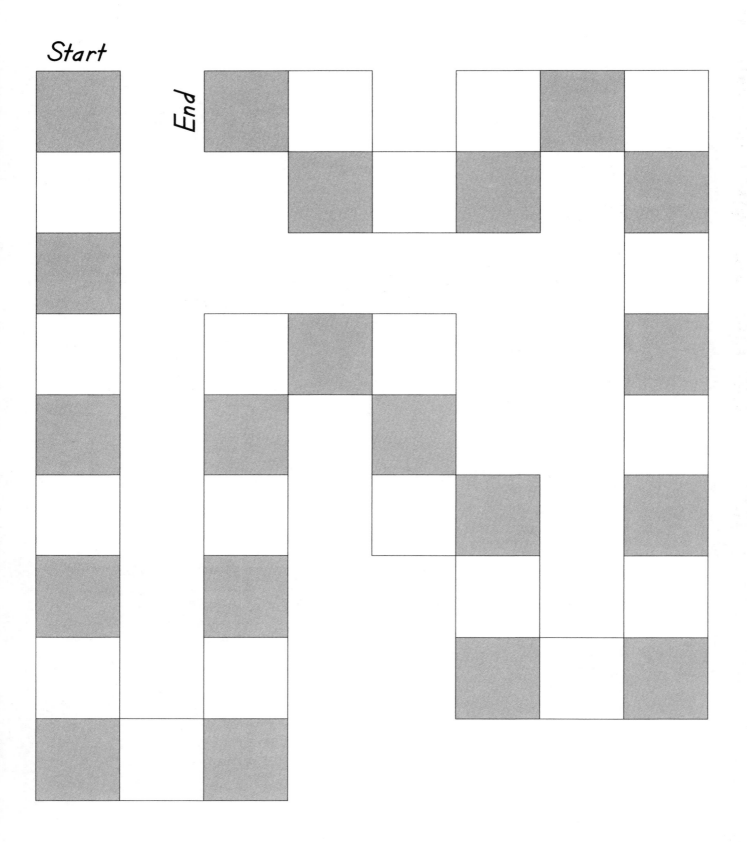

Word Search

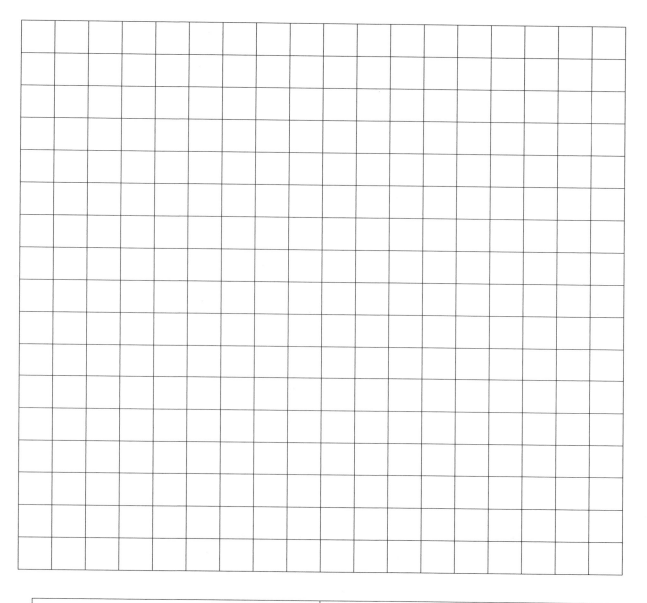

Sink & Spell

	1	2	3	4	5	6	7	8	9	10	11	12	13	14	15	16	17
A																	
B																	
C																	
D																	
E																	
F																	
G																	
H																	
I																	
J																	
K																	
L																	
M																	
N																	

Spelling Tic-Tac-Toe

Spelling Crossword

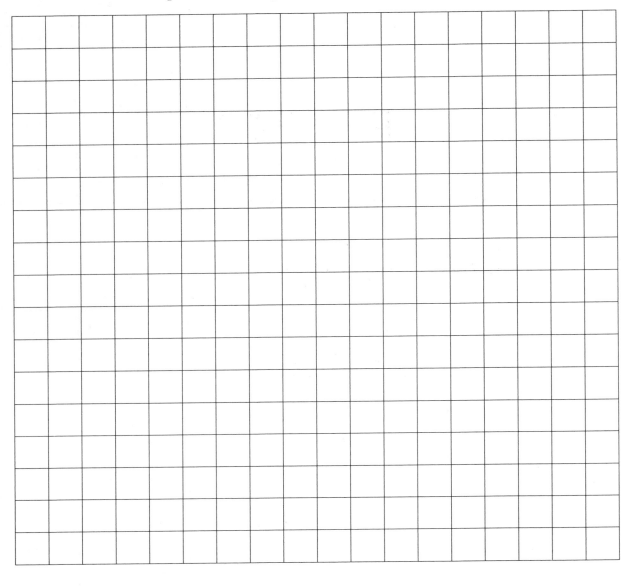

Phonogram Bingo

and

Tic-Tac-Toe Cards

Phonogram Bingo

A-Z Card 1

i	a	p	r	e
y	o	n	c	qu
j	b	d	s	f
x	k	u	g	h
w	v	l	m	z

Phonogram Bingo

A-Z Card 2

b	r	qu	o	p
s	c	g	f	x
t	h	e	n	v
u	k	l	d	w
i	j	m	y	z

Phonogram Bingo

A-Z Card 3

qu	d	p	o	t
r	l	k	c	j
w	u	b	i	s
a	h	n	e	y
x	z	g	m	v

Phonogram Bingo

A-Z Card 4

r	o	j	b	i
g	n	c	p	e
k	qu	f	u	w
s	a	l	v	d
z	t	y	m	x

Phonogram Bingo

A-Z Card 5

c	b	v	w	e
s	o	a	f	x
n	p	r	d	qu
k	l	j	y	i
t	u	g	h	z

Phonogram Bingo

A-Z Card 6

m	s	x	h	c
y	l	d	i	r
p	a	w	v	z
g	f	t	o	j
u	n	e	b	k

Phonogram Bingo

Multi-Letter Phonograms Card 1

ai	igh	ar	ph	ee
eigh	oi	ou	ch	ed
er	bu	ey	au	gu
ng	augh	kn	ear	ir
ck	dge	ea	gn	tch

Phonogram Bingo

Multi-Letter Phonograms Card 2

wr	ow	igh	oe	sh
er	ng	tch	ur	ee
oa	dge	wh	eigh	oo
ay	th	ew	or	bu
augh	ck	ar	ch	ai

Phonogram Bingo

Multi-Letter Phonograms Card 3

sh	gu	oy	ed	ie
ew	ear	ai	eigh	wor
si	dge	igh	au	cei
oa	aw	bu	oa	ur
ti	kn	oi	ch	wh

Phonogram Bingo

Multi-Letter Phonograms Card 4

wor	ough	er	oy	th
eigh	ng	wh	oa	cei
ee	si	oi	ui	ey
ir	ed	ph	ck	or
aw	ie	ea	gn	bu

Phonogram Bingo

Multi-Letter Phonograms Card 5

oy	augh	wr	ay	oe
ei	wh	oo	ch	tch
ough	sh	ui	er	si
ed	or	th	ey	ci
ir	ea	dge	gu	ng

Phonogram Bingo

Multi-Letter Phonograms Card 6

ei	ch	oa	ea	ay
ci	oi	aw	kn	ui
or	er	dge	ed	ie
th	au	gn	ai	ph
ough	ew	oy	si	igh

Phonogram Bingo

Multi-Letter Phonograms Card 7

ee	oo	oe	ie	ay
wr	ar	ch	kn	ir
eigh	ou	augh	ear	gu
wh	ew	dge	ow	ph
ui	ci	th	gn	si

Phonogram Bingo

Multi-Letter Phonograms Card 8

wr	igh	ie	gu	th
ir	wor	kn	ti	ng
or	oo	wh	oi	oe
ough	tch	ou	ur	oa
si	sh	ph	oy	ui

Phonogram Bingo

Multi-Letter Phonograms Card 9

gn	wr	wor	wh	ei
ai	ey	ar	ee	au
bu	ay	ew	aw	augh
ch	ed	cei	er	ci
ear	ea	dge	ck	eigh

Phonogram Bingo

Multi-Letter Phonograms Card 10

cei	ci	ck	dge	aw
ea	ch	ear	augh	ed
ee	ei	au	eigh	er
ew	ar	ey	bu	gn
ai	gu	ie	igh	ay

Phonogram Bingo

Multi-Letter Phonograms Card 11

oa	wor	wr	ie	or
wh	ng	ur	oo	ui
oy	ow	kn	ough	ou
ph	oi	sh	ir	si
oe	tch	th	ti	igh

Phonogram Bingo

Multi-Letter Phonograms Card 12

ai	er	sh	ir	ci
aigh	ay	ough	ou	ow
si	ur	oi	ti	ear
ch	wor	wr	oy	aw
ei	eigh	ey	tch	au

Phonogram Tic-Tac-Toe

A-Z 1

e	d	c
f	a	m
g	h	l

f	c	z
m	a	r
s	qu	t

u	o	w
g	z	k
qu	v	r

z	i	e
w	a	k
o	u	y

Phonogram Tic-Tac-Toe

A-Z 2

b	g	d
l	c	f
k	h	j

m	qu	p
w	n	r
s	t	v

v	r	t
c	d	b
y	z	x

a	r	z
t	e	p
s	o	x

Phonogram Tic-Tac-Toe

A-Z 3

a	qu	e
m	d	o
k	i	g

s	g	y
f	u	d
z	b	w

b	h	f
o	d	j
m	k	qu

s	x	v
z	u	a
m	l	qu

Phonogram Tic-Tac-Toe

A-Z 4

d	m	k
r	g	qu
w	u	t

f	e	x
j	w	l
c	s	z

z	m	l
t	s	h
v	w	r

u	y	i
o	a	t
d	b	e

Phonogram Tic-Tac-Toe

Multi-Letter Phonograms 1

ai	bu	th
ng	or	wh
er	gu	ch

oo	ck	gu
dge	ou	wor
wr	ay	aw

oa	ui	aw
oe	au	ou
ey	ei	ow

th	sh	wh
ough	igh	ph
augh	eigh	tch

Phonogram Tic-Tac-Toe

Multi-Letter Phonograms 2

ai	ou	oy
ui	ay	ow
ey	ei	oi

ai	cei	au
ch	ar	bu
augh	aw	ay

cei	ch	dge
ee	ck	ear
ei	ed	ea

ey	ee	ei
ear	ew	eigh
ea	ed	er

Phonogram Tic-Tac-Toe

Multi-Letter Phonograms 3

gn	ir	igh
kn	gu	ng
oa	oe	ie

kn	aw	gn
ew	dge	au
ck	eigh	ng

oa	oi	oo
or	oe	ou
oy	ow	ough

ough	oo	oa
ow	oe	ou
oi	oy	or

Phonogram Tic-Tac-Toe

Multi-Letter Phonograms 4

ph	tch	si
ur	sh	ti
ui	th	wh

wh	ur	wr
ui	wor	ti
th	tch	si

ci	si	tch
ea	ch	sh
ee	ti	oi

oa	oi	oy
ou	oe	ow
ay	ai	ei

Phonogram Tic-Tac-Toe

Multi-Letter Phonograms 5

bu	igh	augh
ough	gu	wh
ph	sh	eigh

ng	er	gn
wr	kn	ur
wh	ir	ear

tch	bu	igh
ie	au	cei
dge	ei	aw

ed	oo	si
or	ow	th
ar	ai	tch